Encyclopædia Britannica

Fascinating Facts

Transportation

PUBLICATIONS INTERNATIONAL, LTD.

629.04 F   30524524790303
Fascinating facts - transportation.

SERIES PICTURE CREDITS:

Academy of Natural Sciences; Allsport U.S.A.; Animals Animals; Art Resources; Donald Baird; John Batchelor; Blackhill Institute; Ken Carpenter; Bruce Coleman, Inc.; Culver Pictures; Kent & Donna Dannen; FPG International; Brian Franczak; Howard Frank Archives/Personality Photos, Inc.; Tony Freeman/PhotoEdit; Douglas Henderson/Museum of the Rockies/Petrified Forest Museum Association; Carl Hirsch; Blair C. Howard; International Stock Photography; Eleanor M. Kish/Canadian Museum of Nature, Ottawa, Canada; Charles Knight/Field Museum of Natural History; Vladimir Krb/Tyrell Museum; T. F. Marsh; NASA; Gregory Paul; Paul Perry/Uniphoto; Christian Rausch/The Image Works; Peter Von Sholly; SIU/Custom Medical Stock Photo; Daniel Varner; Bob Walters; Peter Zallinger/Random House, Inc.

Beasts of Burden

▶

In earlier times, people tamed and trained animals to haul loads and carry riders. Some are still used today. In Tibet, for example, the yak was used. Desert people train and use the camel because it can endure extreme heat and travel for days without food and water. Its broad padded feet keep it from sinking into the sand. The elephant proved to be a powerful, intelligent pack animal used in the Indian subcontinent. Huskies, bred originally by the Inuit (Eskimos), are still used for pulling sleds in the Arctic.

A Very Strong Camel

A Bactrian (two-humped) baggage camel is very strong. It can carry a load of 600 pounds (270 kg).

People Carriers

The litter or palanquin was a vehicle used to transport people quickly through crowded or narrow streets unsuitable for wheeled vehicles or over rough country where animals were unavailable. It consisted of a box open at one side with a mattress inside on which the occupant reclined. Poles were attached to each end for porters, which could be human or animal.

Early Transport Vehicles ▲

Chariots were probably first used in royal funeral processions. Later, their use was expanded to include farming work and military purposes. The chariot revolutionized warfare by enabling armies to move faster and further than ever before. In surprise attacks, projecting scythes were sometimes fixed to the wheel hubs. Enemy troops advancing on foot would be cut to pieces. Survivors would be felled by the spears, arrows, or swords of soldiers riding beside the chariot-drivers.

An Old-fashioned Taxi

The Sedan chair was a seat in a box with a door and windows for the occupant to see out. It became popular in London and other cities in Europe and North America in the 17th and 18th centuries. It was carried by two to four men and could be hired in the street like a modern taxi.

Travel on the Santa Fe Trail ▶

The Conestoga wagon originated in Pennsylvania in the 18th century and was used on the Santa Fe Trail to carry settlers and their possessions. It had a curved floor to prevent the load (of up to 7 tons (6 tonnes)) from shifting, wheels up to 6$\frac{1}{2}$ feet (2 m) high, and a white canvas cover supported on hoops to 11 feet (3$\frac{2}{5}$ m) above the ground. It was pulled by four or six horses, mules, or oxen.

Travel with Rest Stops ▲

Stagecoaches were coaches that traveled in stages between inns, where travelers could rest and the horses and drivers could be changed. They carried passengers and their luggage. Stagecoaches were most popular between 1820 and 1850, by which time they were superseded by railroads.

Different Kinds of Carriages

Among carriages popular in the 19th century were the barouche (a four-wheeled open carriage), the victoria (a hooded carriage), and the dogcart (in which the passengers sat sideways, back to back).

Delivering the Mail

The Pony Express was a famous trans-American postal service that used a relay of horses and riders from Missouri to California between April 1860 and October 1861. It was set up by the firm of Russell, Majors, and Waddell. Along the trail they built 190 stations, or one about every 10 to 15 miles (16 to 24 km). Five hundred horses were placed at these stations to be used to relieve tired animals. Relief riders also waited at these stations. The first pony express left St. Joseph, Missouri, on April 3, 1860 and arrived in Sacramento, California, on April 13. The Pony Express lasted only 18 months—the telegraph system between the East and the West was completed on October 24, 1861. During its time, horses and riders had covered 616,000 miles (990,000 km) over the 2,000-mile (3,200-km) trail.

Uncomfortable Early Railroads

On the first railroads in the 1800s, the roadbeds, on which the tracks rested, were crudely built and there were no shock absorbers. The cars were wooden and the seats and bunks were hard. Lighting came from either flickering candles or lanterns. In cold weather, the wind blew through the cracks in the car. If there was any form of heating it could only be felt within close range of the wood or coal stoves that were used. Smoke, soot, and sparks flew around and sometimes clothes or cars were set on fire.

Freight Cars Galore

Freight cars vary greatly. There are tank cars for liquids such as milk, oil, and chemicals; refrigerated cars carry fruit, vegetables, meat, and other perishable goods. There is even "piggyback service" in which huge trucks and trailers are loaded on flatcars for transporting over long distances. At the end of their rail journey, the trailers are driven to their final destination.

The First Transcontinental Railway ▲

In 1863, work on the first American transcontinental railroad was started. The Union Pacific started building west from Omaha, Nebraska, and the Central Pacific (now the Southern Pacific) built east from Sacramento, California. On May 10, 1869, the work forces of the two companies met and the rails were joined at Promontory, Utah, in a ceremony that drove a golden spike.

Innovations on the Rails ◄

Sleeping cars were introduced in Great Britain in 1873 for first-class passengers traveling between London and Edinburgh. Four-berth sleepers for second-class passengers were introduced in 1928. Restaurant cars were started in the United States in 1867, but since there were no corridors the passengers in the restaurant car had to remain there throughout the journey.

The Importance of Trains ▶

Trains were once the primary means that got people from place to place. Long-distance trains carried people across the country; other trains carried people from city to city. Goods were also moved from place to place by train.

High-speed Trains
▼

In France and Japan, trains that can go up to 200 miles per hour (322 kph) race people from one end of the country to another. Trains are also used to carry people the short distances between most European cities.

Luxury on the Tracks

The Orient Express was a luxury train that ran from Paris, France, to Istanbul, Turkey, from 1883 to 1977. It was equipped with every comfort its makers could imagine—from Oriental carpets to wood-paneled compartments to velvet draperies. Even the food had a reputation for being the best in the world. Many writers used the train as a setting for novels and short stories, and by the 1920s, the train had become a symbol of "the high life" and the world of drama and adventure. Jet air travel, however, finally put an end to the route. Recently, luxury trains catering to the rich and adventurous are being run on parts of the old Orient Express tracks. These trains are giving the people of today a taste of what was once the most glamorous way to travel.

Getting People to Work ▲

In North America, private cars, airplanes, and trucks have pretty much replaced trains as a means of long-distance transportation. Trains are used, though, to get commuters to and from work each day.

Trains Underground

The term "subway" is usually used for underground trains like the ones found in New York, London, and Paris. Other commuter trains run above the ground—usually on tracks that are elevated above the surface of the city's streets. These elevated trains have been called els for many years. Many subways include above-ground sections that are elevated above road level. As you might expect, these are still called subways.

Noiseless Subways

Subways in cities such as New York and Chicago are noisy because steel wheels run on steel tracks. In some cities, however, subway cars are made with rubber or plastic wheels that run very quietly. These silent wheels and the quiet electric power that most subways use make some subways almost noiseless.

Trains were once the primary means of transportation.

Getting Around by Streetcar

Streetcars were vehicles that were pulled by horses or moved along on their own power. Many of them used electric power and were connected either to an electric rail on the ground or to an overhead wire that carried electricity. Streetcars are still used in many cities, including San Francisco, where cable cars get people up and down the steepest hills.

Let's Take a Taxi

The word "taxicab" comes from two different terms. The first, "taximeter," was used to describe a machine, invented in the 1890s, that automatically figured out how much a passenger had to pay for a ride. The machine measured the distance traveled and then multiplied it by the cost of the ride per mile. The other term, "cabriolet," described a roomy vehicle used to carry passengers around the city. Saying "taximeter-equipped cabriolet" was obviously too much for anyone, so the term "taxicab" was born.

Bicycle Riding Through the Ages

Bicycles have been around since the 1800s when an odd-looking machine called the *draisienne* appeared in Paris, France. It was made of wood, and the rider moved its two wheels along by simply paddling his or her feet against the ground. It was not until the 1890s that modern-style bicycles appeared. When they did, bicycles became hugely popular. Even today, in many parts of the world, millions of people use them as daily transportation.

Special Bikes for Racing

There isn't much difference between racing bikes and everyday bicycles. Racing bikes, however, are very light in weight and are often made from unusual metals like titanium. They also have very expensive gear mechanisms to help riders get up and down hills. Racing bikes have thinner, narrower tires than regular bikes, too. These tires puncture easier than regular tires, but they let riders go much faster. The biggest difference between racing and regular bikes, though, is the riders. Bicycle racers are highly trained, strong athletes who can simply pedal much harder and much faster than the rest of us.

Old-fashioned Bikes of Many Sizes

Many of the bicycles of the 1870s and 1880s had giant front wheels and very tiny rear wheels. Some had front wheels that were more than 5 feet (1.5 m) in diameter—riders had to actually use ladders to get onto their bikes. They were built this way because each turn of the pedals moved this huge front wheel all the way around, causing the bike to travel a great distance on each turn of the pedals. Unfortunately, these bikes were very difficult to ride and often tipped over. Riding them took a great deal of skill and courage.

A Brand-new Tire

A great bicycle invention was J.B. Dunlop's pneumatic tire, introduced in England in 1888.

The Bicycle Craze

The bicycle was very popular in the United States and Europe during the 1890s. Everyone who could afford to buy a bike owned one. On weekdays, the streets were filled with cyclists going to and from work.

Cycle Innovations ▲

In the last century, bicycles have been improved in many ways, including the use of the free wheel, variable-speed gears, lighter wheels and tires, stronger and lighter steel, weatherproofing, better brakes and lighting, better placing of the rider for using his legs to push the pedals, and saddle designs for comfort and speed. The small-wheel bicycle invented by the British engineer Alexander Moulton and introduced in 1962 proved popular and was successful because of its rubber suspension.

◄ Functional and Fun

In Europe and Asia, the bicycle remains an important means of transportation during the 20th century. In the United States and most of Europe, however, the automobile quickly surpassed it as the primary means of transportation. During the late 20th century, bicycling has again enjoyed renewed popularity as a pollution-free means of transportation and as a healthful form of exercise.

Order on the Roads

Traffic laws began before there were even gasoline-powered cars! There have always been rules for horses and carriages. By the 1600s, many European cities had laws making it illegal to park on some streets. In 1865, the famous Locomotives (or "Red Flag") Act was passed. It was designed to do something about the people who were speeding on country and city roads in their steam-powered vehicles. The law set a speed limit of 4 miles per hour (6 kph) on country roads and 2 miles per hour (3 kph) on city roads. It also declared that a person had to walk ahead of any car and wave a red flag to warn people that an automobile was coming. By the 1890s, there were too many vehicles on the roads to make it possible to enforce the law any longer. It was repealed in 1896.

Roads Old and New

People have built roads since the times of the ancient Egyptians. In fact, the ancient Romans were probably the greatest road builders of all time. In the United States, many roads were built in the 1800s to carry wagons, carriages, and horses. When automobiles came along, they were forced to use these rough, dirt roads. Paved roads were introduced as early as the 1850s, but, until automobiles began whizzing along, they were few and far between.

The Original Highway

The first really modern highway created especially for automobiles was the Bronx River Parkway in New York. Built in 1925, it was designed to let cars travel at high speeds without stopping. After that, modern highways and turnpikes sprang up all over the world.

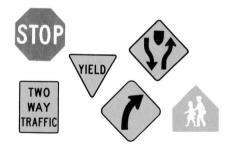

Different Fuels for Automobiles

Kerosene, natural gas, and even hydrogen have all been tried as automobile fuels. Most recently, engineers have been trying to use solar power. Energy from the sun would make cars pollution-free and would save precious fuel. A race is held in Australia every year to find the fastest solar-powered vehicle in the world.

Moving On its Own

A steam-powered tricycle built by Frenchman Nicolas-Joseph Cugnot in 1769 was the first vehicle built that moved along under its own power. It was powerful enough to carry up to four passengers at speeds of 2.25 miles per hour (3.6 kph).

An Automobile First

In the 1880s, the first automobile with a gasoline engine was created by Carl Benz of Germany. He patented his car in 1886, and his name is still on one of the world's most famous cars—the Mercedes-Benz.

The Original Model T ▲

Designed by Henry Ford and sold by the Ford Motor Company in 1908, the Model T was the car that made automobiles affordable for almost everyone. Model T's were so sturdy and simple to repair that many of them remained in daily use for 50 years or more. When it was finally taken out of production in 1927, over 15 million Model T's had been sold.

A Model T Replacement ▼

In 1927, the Ford Motor Company produced a second car to replace the Model T. It was called the Model A.

Electric Automobiles ▲

Electricity was used to power cars as far back as the 1880s. In fact, electric cars were fairly popular up until the 1920s. Power for the cars came from large storage batteries. The cars could run along at a fairly low speed, until the batteries ran out of "juice." Then the cars had to be plugged into a recharger so the batteries could regain their power. Electric cars were most popular among people who did not need to get anywhere in a hurry and who enjoyed having a completely silent automobile.

Gasoline Wins over Steam

The very earliest automobiles—as far back as the 1700s—were powered by steam. Even in the late 1800s, dozens of different companies made steam-powered cars, since it was the easiest way to make a car go. Finally, the safety, low price, and ease of operation of gasoline-powered cars began to drive customers away from the complicated steam cars.

Steam-powered Automobiles ▲

The Stanley "Steamer" was one of the most famous early automobiles. It was built by a company started by twin brothers Francis and Freelan Stanley, and it was manufactured for almost 25 years—from 1897 to 1921.

Automobile Facts ▶

Today's average car is made up of over 14,000 separate parts! They range from simple knobs to complicated electronic circuit boards and are made of everything from plastic to steel to silicon.

Built for a King

The world's most expensive car is the Bugatti Royale, built in the 1920s by Ettore Bugatti. The car was so expensive that Bugatti announced that only those people with royal titles would be allowed to purchase it. Unfortunately, the prices were too high even for kings, queens, and princes. Only a few of the cars were actually sold. Today, the few Bugatti Royales left are selling for millions of dollars each.

This Porsche turbo is an amazingly fast car.

Fastest Cars in the World

For the past ten or 15 years, the cars from three manufacturers—Porsche, Ferrari, and Lamborghini—have generally been considered the fastest cars in the world, with models that reach speeds of just under 200 mph (320 kph). Certain custom-built cars and racing machines, of course, are capable of even higher speeds.

Ferrari 308 GTS

Automobile Racing Firsts

People started racing automobiles almost as soon as they had them. By 1894, carefully organized races were being held in Europe. In 1895, dozens of cars ran in a race between Paris and Bordeaux, France. The event proved so popular that it was held every year until 1903, when the high number of accidents forced the organizers to cancel this race forever. By 1900, races were being held all over the world, with cars reaching speeds of up to 50 mph (80 kph). Thousands of people turned out whenever these machines took to the road.

Rolling Along

Because trucks often carry such heavy loads, they can be very difficult to stop once they get rolling down a hill. (Think of how hard it is to stop a bike that is traveling on a long, steep hill.) Drivers often have to use their brakes and gears to slow the truck down and keep it from running wildly down a hill. That's why highway departments give truck drivers lots of warning about a long, dangerous hill.

Truck Trivia

The first modern truck was built in 1896 by Gottlieb Daimler, the German carmaker whose company became the creator of the famous Mercedes-Benz automobiles. Daimler's truck had a four-horsepower engine and two forward speeds. In 1898, the American Winton Company made a truck especially designed to work as a delivery wagon.

Trucks that Tow

A tractor trailer is a truck that uses a separate towing vehicle that can be attached to a long body (a semitrailer or "semi") in which things are to be carried. The two units are connected together by what is called the "fifth wheel," a latching mechanism that allows the two parts to turn separately while keeping them from coming apart.

Let's Take a Sled Ride

Sleds are used for many things besides riding down hills on a snowy day. In Siberia, Alaska, and Canada's Northwest Territories, dogsleds have been used for hundreds of years. Most are pulled by teams of 12 to 15 dogs.

Sliding Through the Snow

A toboggan has a smooth surface—usually wood—that slides along the surface of the snow. The first toboggans were invented by American Indians, who made them of poles tied together with strips of leather. The Indians used toboggans for getting from place to place during the winter months. Later, people began riding toboggans down hills for sport. By the early 1900s, toboggans were used almost exclusively for fun, as tobogganing became one of the most popular winter sports in the world.

Versatile Snowmobiles ▲

Most snowmobiles are used just for fun. They take people on thrilling rides across the snow and ice, get hunters and fishermen to the best spots in the dead of winter, and help people see places they never could get to otherwise. But they are also useful. In Alaska and Canada's Northwest Territories, they are used to get people from place to place. They are even used by police for everything—from rescue work to chasing criminals.

That's a Fast Machine ▲

Today's lightweight bobsleds can reach speeds of up to 100 mph (160 kph). These bobsleds have streamlined bodies and move on four runners that skim over the surface of the hard-packed snow of the bobsled run. The fastest bobsleds use four riders; two-rider sleds are slightly slower.

A Very Ancient Sport

Scientists have found early skis that are probably between 4,000 and 5,000 years old. These skis, discovered in Sweden and Finland, were most likely made by hunters.

Skiing for All Occasions ▲

Skiing has always been used as a means of transportation. A 4,000-year-old rock carving that was found in Norway, for example, shows two men skiing. They were probably hunting, and their skis were the best way to travel across the snow. The Vikings used skis for hunting and war back in the 10th and 11th centuries. Skis were even used by soldiers during World War II. Today, people still use skis to get from place to place in those parts of the world that remain covered with snow for much of the year. For the most part, though, people ski for fun—and for the excitement of rushing down a hill at top speed.

The Place to Race Is . . .

By the 1860s, ski races were being held in places as far apart as Tromso, Norway, and California.

A Downhill Kind of Race ▲

Cross-country skiing is when people travel from place to place on their skis. They go up and down hills, across flat areas, and through forests. Downhill skiing, sometimes called Alpine skiing, involves a bit of jumping as well. Skiers use the steepness of a hill to give them speed. For this reason, downhill skiing usually means going to a ski slope that has some kind of lift that can take skiers back up to the top of the hill whenever they want to start a run.

Balancing at 100 mph

A boat has to be going at about 20 miles per hour (32 kph) before a water-skier can get up out of the water and onto his or her skis. Expert skiers, though, are able to keep their balance at speeds of up to 100 mph (160 kph).

A Tricky Board on Wheels

Skateboarding first appeared in southern California during the 1960s as a way for surfers to practice and have a good time during bad weather. The surfers simply attached roller skate wheels to pieces of wood that they shaped into tiny surfboards. The result was a fast-moving machine that could turn quickly, race along at high speeds, and even be made to do tricks. By 1965, hundreds of people were skateboarding around the roads and parking lots near California's best beaches. Within a few years, the skateboard was being seen all over the world.

Skating on Wheels

A Belgian named Joseph Merlin is considered to be the inventor of the roller skate. But Merlin's skates, which appeared in the 1760s, did not work very well. In 1863, however, James Plimpton, of Medford, Massachusetts, created the first four-wheeled skates. These skates let riders move faster, stay on their feet better, and create fancy tricks. By the 1890s, there were roller skating rinks all over the country.

The Fastest Skates

Although people can move very rapidly on ice skates, roller skates are generally much faster. The spinning plastic balls on the bottom of the skates allow people to move at much greater speeds than the blades of ice skates, which must cut a thin groove on the surface of the ice.

Shall We Ice Skate? ▲

Ice skating has been around for almost 3,000 years. It has always been done mostly for fun and recreation, even though skates do help people get from place to place. Skating was extremely popular in the 1700s and 1800s, especially among the kings and queens of Europe. It was introduced to North America by British soldiers during the 1740s.

Crossing the Ice by Boat ▼

If you have to cross a large area of ice—a big lake, for example—the best way to go is by iceboat. An iceboat is simply a sailboat with thin blades, or runners, fixed to the sides. A third blade, used for steering, is put at the front or back of the boat. Iceboats, which have been around for more than 2,000 years, can reach speeds up to four times as fast as the wind that is pushing them along. Speeds of 140 miles per hour (220 kph) have been recorded.

Trendy Roller Skaters ▲

In the 1970s, new plastic wheels were put on roller skates. This made the skates faster, smoother, and easier to maneuver. Roller skating became very popular. Later, these same plastic wheels were put on skateboards, helping to make that sport even more popular than ever.

54E 5359

Crossing the Open Seas

A ship is a large floating vessel that can cross open waters. A boat is a much smaller craft.

A History of Ships

Egyptian drawings made about 6000 B.C. show the earliest known ships. The ships in these pictures were made of reeds and were crescent-shaped. The first ones were rowed; later, large square sails were added. By 1500 B.C., ships were common enough for the people of Crete to build them for war and for carrying people and things from place to place. Most early ships used sails, although many also used rowers to power the craft when the wind was light.

Egyptian sailboat

Almost as Fast as Lightning

The *Flying Cloud* was one of the most famous clipper ships of all time. It sailed from New York to San Francisco in just 89 days. Another famous clipper, the *James Baines*, set a record by sailing across the Atlantic Ocean in 12 days and six hours. The *Lightning*, however, was probably the fastest clipper ship of all. It set an all-time record traveling 436 nautical miles (807 km) in a single day.

The Glory of Clipper Ships ▶

Experts consider clipper ships to be the greatest sailing ships ever built. Built in the mid-1800s by American shipbuilders, they were long, slim, graceful, and remarkably fast. They were designed especially for speed, because merchants wanted to bring the first tea of the season back from China. Speed was also important for getting mail and supplies back and forth between the East Coast and the California gold fields during the 1849 Gold Rush.

Down the River by Steamship

The first working steamship was built in 1801 by a British engineer, William Symington. His boat towed barges in the canals of Scotland. In 1807, the American inventor Robert Fulton built a steamboat that went up the Hudson River in about one-fourth the time that it usually took in a sailboat.

Floating Relics

The invention of the jet airplane put an end to most travel by ocean liner. By the late 1960s, most of the famous ocean liners were sold and turned into scrap metal, tourist attractions, or even floating schools.

Making Ships Go ▲

Most ships today are powered by diesel engines. A few nuclear-powered ships have been built, but almost all ships still use gasoline as a source of fuel.

Submarine Specifics

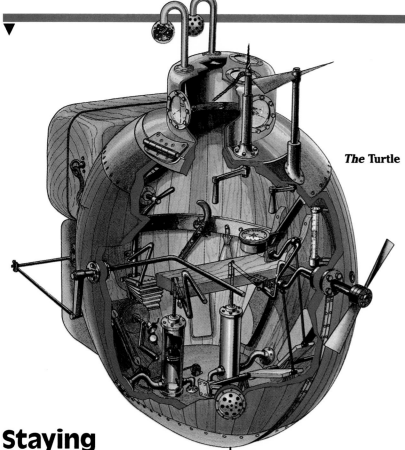

The Turtle

The first working submarine was built in 1776. At that time, an American named David Bushnell built the *Turtle,* a tiny submarine used to attack British ships during the Revolutionary War. Submarines were also used in the 1860s during the American Civil War. By the 1890s, submarines were able to cruise for long distances under the sea.

Staying Underwater

Early submarines could stay underwater for only a short time. By World War II, submarines could stay under for 12 hours or more. There were several reasons why these submarines had to come to the surface: to store air for use under the sea and to recharge the giant batteries that powered the ship underwater. Today's nuclear submarines have solved these problems. As a result, they can stay underwater for weeks and even months at a time.

Fighting Power of Submarines ▲

Submarines have always been used almost exclusively for warfare. They attack surface ships, launch missiles, or set floating bombs (called mines) in areas where they could be hit by passing ships. Submarines are usually too small and too slow to be really useful for carrying cargo or passengers.

Exploring the Bottom of the Sea

Scientists explore the undersea world with a machine called a "bathyscaphe." The bathyscaphe was invented by a Swiss scientist, Auguste Piccard, to study life in the very deepest parts of the ocean. It is made up of a super-strong steel capsule, which holds the divers and scientists. Above this is a tank filled with liquid that is lighter than water. This tank gives the bathyscaphe the "lift" it needs to come back to the surface after it dives. During the 1960s, Piccard's son Jacques set many diving records in the bathyscaphe *Trieste,* eventually reaching a depth of 35,810 ft (10,916 m).

Boats that Fly

"Flying boat" was the term often used for a certain type of seaplane. The entire bottom of a flying boat was designed like a boat, and smaller pontoons, or floats, were attached to the plane's wings. This made it possible for the flying boat to float whenever it was in the water.

Practical Pontoons ▲

The first practical seaplanes were created in 1911 by Glenn Curtiss, an American engineer and pilot. His planes were standard, lightweight planes with large floats, or pontoons, in place of landing wheels. These pontoons kept the plane afloat while it was on the water.

The Heyday of Seaplanes

All through the 1920s and 1930s, the fastest and largest airplanes were seaplanes, which set dozens of records for flights across the Atlantic, the Pacific, and around the world. After World War II, though, planes were able to fly far enough that they no longer had to stop on the water to refuel. As a result, seaplanes were needed only for special uses—like bringing mail or medical help to out-of-the-way places.

▼

Flying on a Cushion of Air

Hovercraft, or air-cushion machines, fly on a cushion of air between the machine and the ground or water surface. Experiments with hovercraft began back in the 1870s, but the first useful air-cushion machine was not built until 1959. This machine, called the SR.N1, was built by Christopher Cockerell of Great Britain and could carry three passengers.

Crossing the English Channel

Hovercraft are primarily being used to carry passengers back and forth across the English Channel. These large hovercraft can carry up to 400 people at speeds of almost 60 knots (70 mph).

A Different Kind of Ferry ▲

A "hydrofoil" is an underwater fin that can lift a ship out of the water. As a ship's speed increases, this fin gradually forces more and more of the boat clear of the water. This allows a ship to move at far greater speeds than it could in the water. During the 1950s, hydrofoil ships began to appear in many parts of the world. Today, they are often used as ferries—even carrying commuters back and forth from the office.

◄ Airfields at Sea

Aircraft carriers are airfields at sea with many special features. To facilitate short takeoffs and landings, airspeeds over the deck are increased by turning the ship into the wind. Catapults flush with the flight deck assist in launching the aircraft. For landing, aircraft are fitted with retractable hooks that engage special wires on the deck, braking them to a quick stop. The control centers of a carrier are situated in a location at one side of the flight deck. Aircraft landings are guided by radio, radar, and hand signals from the deck.

Picking Up Freight

Most ships carry freight. They travel either on regular runs or as "tramps." The tramp steamer carries with it a bit of the romance of the old days of sailing. It wanders from port to port, picking up cargoes and not knowing where it will go next.

Saving Lives at Sea

Modern lifeboats have twin engines for safety reasons. They are fitted with radar, radio, and echo-sounding equipment. They also carry line-throwing apparatus, a breeches buoy (special canvas seat for rescue work), stretcher, first aid equipment, emergency rations, and a scrambling net.

A Ship for Every Purpose ▲

Many ships—oil tankers, for example—are built especially for certain kinds of cargo. Other special ships include refrigerator ships, tugs, lumber schooners, grain ships, ore boats, ventilated ships for tropical fruits, colliers for coal, ferryboats that are usually double-ended, icebreakers that are designed to ride up over the ice and crush it with their weight, and container ships whose cargo is placed inside many large boxes made of aluminum alloy.

Rules on the Seas

The "rule of the road" on the water is that rowing and sculling boats (as well as steam and motor-driven ones) must give way to sailboats, while rowers and scullers out for pleasure or practice must give way to those racing. On a river, the general rule is to keep in the middle when going with the stream and to one side when going against it. On a lake or at sea, two boats traveling in opposite directions should pass port side to port side. (The port side is the left side looking forward; the right side is called the starboard.)

A Long History at Sea ▲

A catamaran is descended from a type of boat that has existed in the Pacific islands for thousands of years. The name comes from the Tamil (southern Indian) word *katta-maram* meaning "tied tree," and was originally used for rafts made by lashing together tree trunks. Nowadays catamarans are craft with the weight equally shared between two hulls.

◀Romantic Gondolas

Gondolas are the best-known means of transportation in Venice, Italy. They are flat-bottomed boats, with raised stern and bows, and are often 30 feet long (9 m). They are usually propelled by one oarsman, the gondolier, who stands at the stern.

Ships of the Air

Dirigibles are large flying machines. The early ones consisted of a compartment for passengers and crew and a giant balloon filled with lighter-than-air gas. Propellers were used to move the ships through the air.

Uses for Dirigibles

During World War I, dirigibles were used for anti-submarine warfare and for bombing London and Paris. By the 1920s, dirigibles were in service for long-distance air travel. German dirigibles were the most successful, with the *Graf Zeppelin* making almost 600 flights. Passengers liked the quiet, stable ride of the airships and did not seem to mind their slow pace. People became concerned about the safety of dirigibles, however, when the hydrogen-filled balloon of the German airship *Hindenberg* exploded in Lakehurst, New Jersey, in 1937. Since then, dirigibles have been used occasionally by armies and air forces. Today, nonrigid dirigibles, or blimps, are used for advertising by companies such as Goodyear Tire & Rubber and Fuji Film. They are also sometimes used for sight-seeing and scientific observation. These blimps are filled with nonflammable helium, making them much safer than the hydrogen dirigibles of the past.

The First Flyers

Flight began when two Americans, Wilbur and Orville Wright, began work on an airplane in 1899. By 1902, they had created a successful two-winged glider. In 1903, the Wrights added a 12-horsepower engine and two propellers. On December 17, 1903, the Wright Brothers' *Flyer* (as they named it) flew for 59 seconds. By 1905, their third *Flyer* was flying, turning, making circles, and staying in the air for up to half an hour at a time. Within a few years, Europeans were also building planes—the age of flight had begun.

From One Wing to Two

In 1909, a single-winged plane became the first airplane to cross the English Channel. Between then and 1914, many of the world's best airplanes had only a single wing. But a number of accidents with monoplanes (as the one-winged airplanes were called) convinced engineers that wings needed a great deal of support. For this reason, they started using two and even three wings, all held together with wood or metal struts and strong wires. These braces managed to hold the fragile wood and fabric planes in the air.

Memorable Atlantic Crossing

Charles Lindbergh was the first person to complete a solo, nonstop flight across the Atlantic Ocean. Although people had crossed the Atlantic before, they had done so by making several stops. Lindbergh, however, left Roosevelt Field, outside New York City, and, a little more than 33 hours later, landed outside of Paris, France. The flight, which took place May 20-21, 1927, captured the public's imagination. Overnight, Lindbergh became one of the most famous and honored people in the world.

A Famous Woman Pilot

The most popular early woman flyer was Amelia Earhart. Earhart had been an army nurse during World War I where she became interested in flying. In 1928, she became famous for flying across the Atlantic Ocean as a passenger. Determined to earn respect as a pilot, she made a series of flights around the United States to attract attention to herself and to the growing airline industry. In 1935, she made a solo flight from Hawaii to California—the first person to ever successfully make that flight. In 1937, she set out to fly around the world. After completing two-thirds of the flight, her plane vanished in the middle of the Pacific Ocean and she was never found.

Flying Around the Globe

On April 6, 1924, four United States Army Air Service planes left Seattle, Washington, in an attempt to become the first to fly around the globe. Although one plane was forced to make a crash landing off the coast of Alaska, and another one was lost in the North Atlantic, two of the planes returned to Seattle 175 days and over 26,000 miles (41,850 km) later.

The Story of Jets

A jet engine works by pushing hot gas out of itself. This gives the engine the power to move things through the air or off the ground. The first jet aircraft was created in Germany, in 1939, just before World War II. By the late 1940s, jets were used in most of the world's air forces, and by 1952, the first jet airliners were in service.

The Job of a Pilot

Either the pilot or copilot is always seated at the controls during every moment of flight. Flight plans must be created, reviewed, and registered for each flight. Weather must be checked constantly so that the plane can avoid dangerous weather conditions. The pilot must also be on the lookout for other aircraft to make sure that there are no midair collisions. A plane's pilot and copilot are also at the controls for most takeoffs and landings, just to make sure that everything goes smoothly. The captain is even in charge of maintaining law and order on the plane—just like a captain on a ship.

The First Commercial Airline

An American named Tony Jannus established the world's first commercial airline in 1914. Jannus's airline, which had a full schedule of flights between St. Petersburg and Tampa, Florida, could carry only one passenger at a time. People, however, were not really ready for air travel at that time, and Jannus's airline went out of business after a few months. After World War I, however, people were more willing to accept the idea of air travel. Slowly, airlines began to be organized, and, by the 1930s, adventurous and wealthy people were traveling by air.

The Busiest Airports

Surprisingly, the busiest airports are not always in the largest cities. Some airports serve as "hubs"—they are used hundreds of times each day by people who change from one plane to another in order to get to where they are going. Someone going from Boston, Massachusetts, to Dallas, Texas, for example, would probably fly from Boston to Atlanta, Georgia. There, he or she would change planes and fly to Dallas. Consistently, Chicago's O'Hare Field and Atlanta's Hartsfield Airport are among the very busiest in the world.

The Effects of Wind

An airliner's progress is affected by the wind. A headwind slows up its speed over the earth, while a tailwind increases speed. A wind blowing from either side causes it to drift to the other side as it travels forward.

Jumbo Jets

The first of the wide-bodied jets, the Boeing 747, has a wing span of 197 feet (60 m) and a length of 185 feet (56.4 m). Powered by four very large turbofan engines, it cruises about 600 miles (970 km) per hour.

The Famous "Black Box"

The so-called "black box" flight recorder automatically records every detail of the flight, and recordings can also be made of conversations on the flight deck. Should anything go wrong, and the aircraft be forced to suddenly land or even crash, these records are invaluable in helping experts to discover the cause of the failure.

Keeping in Contact ▶

An aircraft is hardly ever cut off from contact with the ground, even when it is flying high above the clouds or over the ocean. Radio messages are constantly passing between the airplane and the ground radio stations as the aircraft flies along airways—corridors about 9 miles (15 km) wide that are marked out over land with radio navigation beams. It is the job of the crew to see that the airliner flies along these airways.

Helpful Helicopters

Because they can hover in the air and lift straight off the ground without a runway, helicopters are extremely useful. They are used in warfare to carry troops into battle as well as to attack enemy positions. They are also widely used for rescuing people, especially at sea and in hard-to-reach areas. Today, they are also popular for making short air flights, often from the middle of one city to another. Many passengers, for example, are willing to pay a high price for the privilege of having a helicopter take them from a city's downtown area to a nearby airport.

Helicopter Statistics

The first real helicopter was built by the famous Russian engineer, Igor Sikorsky. By 1910, Sikorsky had built two helicopters, and, within a few years, other people had made their own versions of these flying machines. The first helicopter that was actually good enough to be used for practical tasks was built in Germany during the 1930s. In 1938, Hanna Reitsch flew it and established several world records—proving that helicopters would soon be an excellent form of transportation.

Vertical Takeoff and Landing ▶

Since being able to take off and land without a runway is useful, engineers worked for many years to develop a plane capable of vertical takeoff and landing (VTOL). Several such planes have been made for the world's air forces. However, they are usually not fast enough to be all that practical for passengers.

◄ The Alaskan Pipeline

The trans-Alaska pipeline, completed in 1977, carries petroleum 800 miles (1,300 km) from Prudhoe Bay on Alaska's Arctic coast to the Pacific coast port of Valdez. Work was done over rugged terrain and in Arctic weather and plans had to include ways of preserving the environment. Other uses for pipelines include carrying water from lakes and rivers for irrigation and drinking purposes and transporting coal.

A Very Long Pipeline

One of the longest pipelines in the world is the trans-Siberian, which carries natural gas from northern Siberia approximately 3,750 miles (6,000 km) to western Europe.

A Truly Vast Undertaking

The construction of the Panama Canal took seven years and was directed by John Stevens and George Goethals. Close to 65,000 men were employed at one time, and more than 200 million cubic yards (153 cubic meters) of soil and rock were moved. The canal opened to ships in August 1914, and effectively cut the sailing distance from New York to San Francisco by 8,000 miles (13,000 km).

A Famous Waterway ►

The Panama Canal is a great international waterway connecting the Atlantic and Pacific Oceans through the Isthmus of Panama in Central America. The canal is located near the geographical center of the western hemisphere and is a vital link in the world's ocean trade routes. Just over 11,000 ships pass through its locks each year, saving a vast amount of money in shipping costs by reducing the distances that goods must travel by sea.

Mountain Travel

▶

A form of transportation common in some mountainous areas is the aerial cableway. This uses very strong steel ropes that are winched electrically back and forth onto cable drums, or worked on the "endless belt" principle, similar to the San Francisco cable cars. Where the land allows, the cables may be supported on towers. Cableways are used to pull or carry skiers and tourists up mountain slopes.

Two Types of Monorails

Monorails are single-track rail systems that can carry passengers or freight. They fall into two types. The train may run on top of the rail supported on wheels, an air cushion, or magnetically, or it may be suspended below the rail, supported by its drive wheel.

A Monorail First

The first successful "over-rail" monorail was invented by Charles Lartigue in 1883 and built at Ballybunion, Ireland. It consisted of a twin-boilered steam engine and carriages that ran on wheels, and straddled the rail that was supported on trestles 2 feet (60 cm) above the ground. Loads had to be very carefully balanced to prevent the monorail from overturning. Modern versions are found in Seattle and Tokyo.

Using a Magnetic Field

Magnetic levitation, or "Maglev," has been used for the monorail link to Birmingham International Airport in England. The train is supported above a flat steel rail by a magnetic field. Propulsion is by linear motor—similar to a conventional motor that has been flattened out to give motion in a straight line instead of a circle.

Sketching for the Future

Leonardo da Vinci, the great Italian artist and inventor, made sketches of a man-propelled tank in 1482. It was not until the gasoline engine had been developed, however, that there was a compact source of power able to move a heavy gun and armor about the battlefield.

Tank Duties ▲

The first tanks were developed in World War I (1914-18). They were developed from motorized caterpillar-tracked tractors. In World War I, the task of tanks was to clear a way for the infantry through the barbed-wire entanglements and to overrun trenches and machine-gun positions.

Moving on All Surfaces

In all modern tanks, the engine turns wheels engaging in steel links called tracks on each side. As a result, a tank's weight is spread over the underside of both tracks, giving better grip. Despite a weight of over 55 tons (50 tonnes), the tank can move at speed through mud, snow, rain, or rough terrain.

Modern Tank Capabilities ▲

The main weapon of a tank is its long-barreled and very accurate gun. A "ranging" machine gun is often mounted alongside the big gun. It fires tracer bullets in bursts; these are easily seen so that the gunner can correct the aim of the big gun. A modern tank uses laser beams for range-finding and may also be armed with guided weapons. Its armor is designed to deflect enemy gunfire. Its infra-red system enables the crew to see in the dark, and a filtered air supply allows them to remain inside for up to 72 hours with the hatches closed.